You Know You're A College Student When...

SECOND PRINTING — MAY 1987

ISBN 0-8431-1571-8

You Know You're A College Student When...

Written by Paul Barlow, Jr.
Illustrated by Stephanie O'Shaughnessy

PRICE/STERN/SLOAN
Publishers, Inc., Los Angeles
1987

You know you're a college student when...

you're forced to carry around the worst photo of your life

You know you're
a college student
when...

you meet the world's weirdest human...and he's your roommate

You know you're a college student when…

you START a food fight

You know you're
a college student
when…

you get so homesick you want to quit school 87 times during your freshman year

you wait forever in a drop/add line...

and fail to get even one of the classes you wanted

You know you're a college student when...

you spend your entire financial aid check in 2 days
and not a penny goes for tuition

You know you're
a college student
when...

you spend $48.95 on the wrong edition of a textbook

You know you're a college student when...

you live beneath the person with the worst
<u>and</u> loudest music ever recorded

You know you're
a college student
when...

you send a month's laundry home to Mom via U.P.S.

You know you're a college student when...

you live for months on "Mystery Meat" and "Bug Juice"

You know you're a college student when...

you are forced out into the coldest night of January for a fire drill

You know you're
a college student
when...

you are drowned in the dorm room

You know you're a college student when…

you walk through a blizzard at dawn only to find your class is canceled

You know you're
a college student
when...

you rediscover the time-tested axiom—"The nicer the professor the harder the course"

You know you're
a college student
when...

you try to highlight a text and end up with a yellow book

You know you're a college student when...

you go to a pre-exam <u>help session</u> that doesn't

You know you're
a college student
when...

you wash the dishes and reorganize the closets twice
to avoid studying

You know you're a college student when...

*you go through your entire college career
without seeing your "advisor"*

You know you're
a college student
when...

you blow off an inconsequential final for a crucial all-night Monopoly game

You know you're
a college student
when...

you go to the wrong room in the wrong building at the wrong time for your final

You know you're
a college student
when...

you walk into class after a week's absence to find the professor writing "No Talking During The Exam" on the board

You know you're a college student when...

you take a midterm that covers NOTHING
from your notes or textbook

You know you're a college student when...

you write a five-page essay containing not one fact

You know you're a college student when...

you guess your way through a 50 question multiple-choice quiz

you take a class because it is an easy "A"...

and discover it is the easiest "D" of your life

You know you're a college student when...

you start a term paper the night before it's due

You know you're a college student when…

you hear your parents ask, "Do you think we're spending all this money so you can party for the next 4 years??"

You know you're
a college student
when...

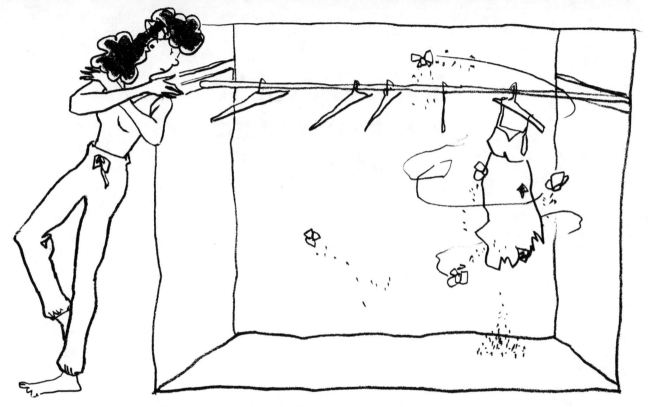

you watch your wardrobe become communal property
in the dorm

You know you're a college student when...

you regularly eat your one meal of the day at a local
"Happy Hour" free hors d'oeuvres buffet

You know you're a college student when...

you unearth the perfect "cruising" spot on campus

You know you're a college student when...

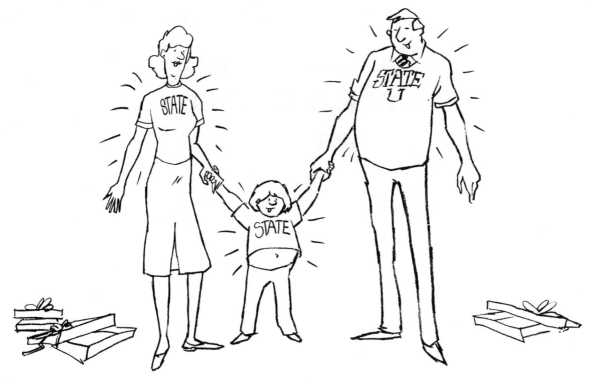

you bring everyone in your family T-shirts emblazoned with your school insignia

You know you're a college student when...

you sacrifice a bedsheet from home for a toga party

You know you're a college student when...

you spend spring break in Ft. Lauderdale having a blast being pushed and shoved by 2 million other college students

You know you're a college student when...

you find a good reason to party on any occasion

you drink 500 gallons of beer and 349 varieties of punch...

in one rush week

You know you're
a college student
when…

you are told about all the embarrassing things you did at a
rush party you can't remember attending

You know you're
a college student
when...

you learn to "drive the porcelain bus"

You know you're
a college student
when...

you think up a perverted name for your intramural softball team

You know you're
a college student
when…

you are asked to join the <u>nerd</u> fraternity

You know you're a college student when...

you toilet paper the President's front yard

You know you're
a college student
when...

*you live in abject poverty so you'll always have plenty
of <u>partying</u> money*

You know you're a college student when...

you overdraw because your parents forgot to deposit the $200.00

You know you're a college student when...

*your phone is disconnected just because you didn't pay
the bill for a few months*

You know you're
a college student
when...

you wait outside in the rain for three days for tickets to a two-hour concert

You know you're
a college student
when...

you realize halfway through senior year that you chose the wrong major

You know you're a college student when...

you catch an incurable case of Senioritis

And furthermore, you REALLY know you're a college student when...

*you're scheduled for 6 classes you don't need to graduate. . .
all at 8 A.M.*

*you find out the book store ran out of your textbook
two days before the midterm*

*you become close personal friends with someone
because she's heard of your hometown*

*you become today's hot gossip over something
you thought no one would find out*

*you kill off several aunts, uncles and other assorted
relatives just as papers are due*

*you lie to your parents about how much better your
grades are this term*